Galway Arts Festival and the Bu

T0258646

trad

by M A R K D O H E R T Y

First performed at the 2004 Galway Arts Festival

Subsequently performed at the Dublin Theatre Festival 2004,
Edinburgh Festival Fringe 2005, and Adelaide Festival 2006

First performed in London at the Bush Theatre on 4 April 2006

**GALWAY
ARTS FESTIVAL**
—— 2006 ——

Company

Son	Peter Gowen
Da	Frankie McCafferty
Sal / Father Rice	David Pearse
Guitar	Tony Byrne
Fiddle	Malachy Bourke
Director	Mikel Murfi
Designer	Paul Keogan
Composer	Jim Doherty
Production Manager	Marie Breen
Stage Manager	Catherine Buffrey
Publicity	Paul Fahy
Producer	Rose Parkinson

Biographies

Mark Doherty
Writer

Radio credits include *Only Slaggin'*, *A Hundred and Something, Stand-up Sketches* and *The Bees of Manulla* for RTE, and *The O' Show* for BBC Radio 4. He has written for, and appeared in, various TV shows, including *The Stand Up Show*, and *Back to the future* for the BBC, and *Couched*, a 6-part comedy series for RTE.

Theatre credits include *Lunch*, by Steven Berkoff, *Accidental Death of an Anarchist*, by Dario Fo, an Abbey production of *The Hostage* by Brendan Behan and *I am the Tiger* written as part of *Car Show* for the Corn Exchange. From 1995 to 2000 Mark worked extensively as a stand-up comedian performing all around Ireland and England, as well as Edinburgh, New York, and Adelaide.

Acting credits include *The Struggle, Headrush, Custer's Last Stand-up, Any Time Now, Rebel Heart, The Magnificent Ambersons, November Afternoon, Angela's Ashes, Disco Pigs, Rat, Ballykissangel, Father Ted, The Clinic, The League of Gentlemen's Apocalypse* and Neil Jordan's film *Breakfast on Pluto*. He recently appeared in *Playin' aRound* for Galway Arts Festival which he wrote, and performed in Barry Murphy's *The Giant* also at the Galway Arts Festival. Mark was the recipient of the 2004 BBC Radio Drama Award (Stewart Parker Award) for *Trad*.

Mikel Murfi
Director

Mikel Murfi is an actor, writer and director from Sligo. He trained at Ecole Jacques Lecoq, Paris. He was a founding member of the company Barabbas, with whom he performed and directed over a period of eight years. As an actor he most recently appeared in *Playin' aRound* which he directed for Galway Arts Festival and played Seanie Murphy in Conal Creedon's *The Cure* at the Half Moon Theatre, Cork. He played *James* in Tom Murphy's *The Morning After Optimism* and *Christy Mahon* in Synge's *The Playboy of the Western World* both at The Peacock Theatre. In the Abbey Theatre he has performed as *Stefano* in *The Tempest* and *Dromio of Syracuse* in *The Comedy of Errors*. With Barabbas, he appeared in eight shows. He played *Martin Kriebal* in *The Increased Difficulty of Concentration* by Vaclav Havel with Druid Theatre Company and multiple roles in the Rough Magic Theatre Company production of Oscar Wilde's *Lady Windermere's Fan*.

Mikel has appeared in many film and television projects including *The Butcher Boy, The Last September* and *Ella Enchanted*. As a writer and director his most recent work has been with Macnas in Galway, including *Diamonds in the Soil* based on the life and works of Vincent Van Gogh, the award winning *The Lost Days of Ollie Deasy*, based on Homer's *Odyssey* and most recently a version of the Medieval Mystery Plays. He teaches on Masters Degree theatre programme in NUI Galway and also in Denmark, Norway and London. He is currently researching a solo theatre show which takes place entirely underwater. Mikel has just directed *The Walworth Force* for Druid Theatre, Galway.

Jim Doherty
Composer

Jim Doherty is probably Ireland's musical man for all seasons. As composer he has written hundreds of radio and TV jingles, and signature tunes from *Seven Days* to *Wanderly Wagon* to *Simply Delicious*. He was the music director of RTE's (Ireland National Broadcasting Service) *The Late Late Show* for ten years. As jazz pianist he has played with the world's best, from Gerry Mulligan to Zoot Sims, and has lectured on the subject at most Irish third-level colleges.

As comedy writer he co-scripted RTE's *Only Slaggin'* for many years. In the theatre, he wrote the music for the Abbey's first musical *Innish*, which is still being performed. Jim has directed many theatre productions, including *Side By Side By Sondheim* and *Jacques Brel Is Alive And Well* for Noel Pearson. He regularly performs at the National Concert Hall in Dublin.

Peter Gowen Son

Peter Gowen began his career with Players Theatre whilst at TCD. His work includes *Arrah-na-Pogue*, *Fathers and Sons*, *Juno and the Paycock* and *Great Expectations* at the Gate; *Whistle in the Dark*, *Observe the Sons of Ulster Marching towards the Somme* and *Communion* at the Abbey; *Werewolves*, *The Country Boy*, *At the Black Pig's Dyke*, *A Touch of the Poet* and *The Beauty Queen of Leenane* with Druid; *Making History* with Field Day; *Translations*, *Death of a Salesman* and *Philadelphia, Here I Come* at the Gaiety; *Bedbound* at the New Theatre for

which he won the Evening Herald and Irish Times/ESB Best Actor Award.

In Britain his work includes *Yerma* at the Manchester Royal Exchange; *Someone to Watch Over Me* and *Royal Supreme* at Theatre Royal, Plymouth; *A Doll's House* and *Abigail's Party* at Theatre Clwyd; The Gate production of *Juno and the Paycock* at the Albery; *The Lieutenant of Inishmore* and *The Plough and the Stars* at the Garrick; *A Doll's House* at the Playhouse; and, on Broadway at the Belasco, *Making History; The Forest* and *Mutabilitie* at the RNT. TV and Film work includes *The Paradise Club*, *On Home Ground*, *Coronation Street*, *Minder*, *The Bill*, *The Jump*, *Trial and Retribution II*, *The Butcher Boy*, *A Love Divided Dancing At Lughnasa* and *Breakfast On Pluto*.

Frankie McCafferty
Da

Frankie tudied at UCG and the Conservatoire National Supérieur d'Art Dramatique, Paris.

Recent theatre includes *Endgame* for Prime Cut Productions at the Waterfront Studio, Belfast to mark the centenary of Samuel Beckett's birth, the world premiere of Daragh Carville's *Family Plot* for Tinderbox Theatre Company, Belfast and Conal Creedon's *Second City Trilogy* at the Half Moon Theatre, Cork.

Other theatre includes *Conversations on a Homecoming* and *Observe the Sons of Ulster Marching towards the Somme* (Irish Times Best Supporting Actor award) at the Belfast Lyric, and *Sharon's Grave* (Irish Times Best Actor nominee) and *At the Black Pig's Dyke* (which toured to London, Toronto and Sydney) for Druid Theatre Company, Galway.

TV includes roles in *The Return* (ITV), *Pulling Moves, Any Time Now, Murder in Eden, Children of the North,* and *Ballykissangel* (in which he appeared in every episode for six seasons) (BBC).

Recent film roles have been in *Omagh* and *Middletown* (currently in post production) and many others including *In the Name of the Father, Sweety Barrett, Fools of Fortune, Angela's Ashes, Guiltrip, Sweeney Todd* and *The Birth of Frank Pop.*

He directed the comedy *The Nativity... What the Donkey Saw* at the Lyric Belfast, and the short films *Brood, Flush, Filleann an Feall (What Goes Around...),* and *The Devil* (based on a short story by Guy de Maupassant).

(Island Theatre Company), *Alone it Stands* (Yew Theatre Company), *Conversation with a Cupboard Man* (Semper Fi), *Diurmuid and Gráinne* and *Studs* (Passion Machine). He was awarded Best Actor in the 2001 Dublin Fringe Festival in *Scenes From a Watercooler* (Guna Nua Theatre Company).

He appeared most recently in *The Shaughraun* (The Abbey Theatre), *Life of Galileo* (Rough Magic Theatre) and *The Playboy of the Western World* (Druid). Film and television work includes: *Spin the Bottle, Rebel Heart* (BBC), *An Everlasting Piece* (Dreamworks), *Bloody Sunday, Bachelor's Walk, Laws of Attraction* and *Homeland* (The Abbey Theatre).

David Pearse
Sal / Father Rice

David first started acting with the Viewpoint Players in Newry with Seán Hollywood. David's first play with Seán was *A Midsummer Night's Dream* in which he played *Demetrius*. He studied drama at the Samuel Beckett Centre, Trinity College Dublin. His appearances include *The Hunt for Red Willie* (nominated Best supporting actor in 2000 Irish Times/ ESB Theatre Awards), *At Swim Two Birds, Lolita* (in cooperation with The Corn Exchange), *Henry IV Part One* (Abbey and Peacock Theatres), *The Misanthrope* and *Eccentricities of a Nightingale* (The Gate), *Mud* (Best Production 2003 Irish Times/ESB Theatre Awards), *The Seagull, Five-Car Show,* (Corn Exchange), *Feileacán Fáin* (Iomha Idánach), *Julius Caesar, The Revenger's Tragedy, Measure For Measure, The Spanish Tragedy, Coriolanus* and *The White Devil* (Loose Canon Theatre Company), *Borrowed Robes, Carolan's Farewell, Pigtown*

Tony Byrne Guitar

Tony developed an interest in music from an early age and by 14 he was playing drums with a number of different Rock bands. At 16, Tony discovered traditional music in Co. Kerry, and began joining in on the many sessions there. He then began a course in Progressive Traditional And Folk Music Performance which led to the formation of *Shinook*, a band comprised of fellow students. With *Shinook* Tony was able to stretch his guitar skills to the limit while touring around Europe and Ireland. Tony has since recorded and toured with a number of different bands and artists, bringing his unique, subtle guitar playing to fresh audiences around the world. He is currently working with John McSherry in *At First Light*, with the prospect of more exciting albums to come.

Malachy Bourke
Fiddle

Malachy Bourke was born in Co. Galway. He was raised listening to some of the best traditional Irish musicians in one of the most artistically buoyant regions in the world. From the age of nine he was being taught fiddle by master musician Frankie Gavin. Since moving to Dublin at the age of eighteen he has pursued a varied and interesting career, touring in Ireland, the UK, Europe and North America, freelance and with groups such as the Irish Pure Drops, Sessions from the Hearth, Tony Kenny's Ireland and Jury's Irish cabaret. Malachy has also worked in film and on several seasons with the reputable dance company Rubato Ballet. Malachy's solo cd *Draw the Bow* has been well received worldwide and he is currently working on a duet cd with Uilleann piper Donnacha Dwyer called simply *Bourke and Dwyer*, due for release in early summer it will be launched in both Ireland and Germany.

Paul Keogan
Designer (Lighting & Set)

Born in Dublin, Paul studied Drama at The Samuel Beckett Centre, Trinity College Dublin and at Glasgow University. After graduating he worked as Production Manager for Project Arts Centre. His designs include: *Melonfarmer, The Electrocution of Children, Living Quarters, Making History, Mrs Warren's Profession, Bailegangáire, The Tempest, Tartuffe, Eden, That Was Then, Da, The Wild Duck, The Cherry Orchard, The Burial at Thebes, Defender of the Faith, Portia Coughlan* and *Heavenly Bodies* (Abbey and Peacock Theatres); *Down Onto Blue, Danti Dan, Olga* and *Sugar Wife* (Rough Magic); *Gates of Gold* and *Performances* (Gate Theatre); *Born Bad* and *In Arabia We'd All Be Kings* (Hampstead Theatre, London); *Too Late for Logic* (Edinburgh International Festival); *Shimmer* and *Olga* (Traverse Theatre, Edinburgh); *The Tempest* (Theatre Royal, Plymouth); *The Silver Tassie*, (Almeida Theatre, London); *Chair, Angel Babel* and *Passades* (Operating Theatre); *Quay West, Blasted* and *Far Away* (Bedrock Productions); *Blue/Orange* (Crucible Theatre, Sheffield). Paul's designs for Dance include: *Sweat* and *Beautiful Tomorrow* (ManDance); *Ballads, Seasons* and *The Rite of Spring* (CoisCéim); *Macalla* and *Intimate Gold* (Irish Modern Dance Theatre); *SAMO* (Block & Steel, Netherlands) and *Catalyst*, a collaboration between Rex Levitates and The National Ballet of China in Beijing.

Opera designs include: *Tosca, Jenufa, The Queen of Spades, Madama Butterfly, Lady Macbeth of Mtensk, The Silver Tassie, Gianni Schicchi* and *A Florentine Tragedy* (Opera Ireland); *The Lighthouse* (Opera Theatre Company); *The Makropulos Case, Un Ballo in Maschera* and *Der Fliegende Holländer* (Opera Zuid, Netherlands). Paul also designed *The Wishing Well*, a large-scale outdoor projection piece for Kilkenny Arts Festival 1999, designed lighting for the Irish Pavilion at the Architectural Biennale in Venice and most recently designed *Here Lies* by Operating Theatre for Galway Arts Festival. Paul is an associate artist of the Abbey Theatre, Dublin.

Galway Arts Festival

GALWAY
ARTS FESTIVAL
2006

Situated on the west coast of Ireland by the Atlantic Ocean Galway has been long considered Ireland's capital of culture. The fastest growing city in Europe, with a population of 75,000, Galway is a young and vibrant university city.

Galway Arts Festival is the defining cultural expression of Galway and is at the heart of all aspects of life in the city. As the Festival celebrates Galway in July each year, Galway itself is a city in celebration during the Festival. Galway Arts Festival contributes immeasurably to the economic, social and cultural life of the west of Ireland.

Over its 28 year history the Festival has become a vital showcase for Irish arts internationally and international arts in Ireland and is now firmly established as Ireland's leading arts festival. The Festival collaborates with artists and companies throughout the world to produce, create, present and commission new work.

Regarded as one of Europe's key cultural events Galway Arts Festival is an international two-week celebration of the performing and visual arts. Over 100,000 people attend the Festival annually, with hundreds of writers, artists, performers and musicians from all over the world creating theatre, spectacle, street art, music, comedy, literature and music in a stunning fortnight of cultural activity and celebration.

The spirit of Galway Arts Festival is all-inclusive, accessible and always open to suggestion. Contemporary festivals fall over themselves to state their commitment to both street and 'high art'. The difference in Galway is that ambition is realised. **The Observer**

The biggest, most exciting, most imaginative explosion of arts activity this country has. **The Irish Times**

GALWAY ARTS FESTIVAL

Artistic Director	**Paul Fahy**
Festival Manager	**John Crumlish**
Festival Administrator	**Elizabeth Duffy**
Financial Controller	**Gerry Cleary**
Aministration	**Susan McKenna**

Galway Arts Festival, Black Box Theatre, Galway, Ireland.
+35391509700
www.galwayartsfestival.ie

Trad was originally produced in 2004 by Rose Parkinson for Galway Arts Festival.

Echoes of the Absurd
by Colm Tóibín

GALWAY
ARTS FESTIVAL
——2006——

History, for the characters in Mark Doherty's *Trad*, is the comedy from which they are trying to awake. History may also have been a tragedy, especially when its main events were repeated many times, but the age of tragedy has passed. The play is set in a time when it is hard to know whether to laugh or cry. Someone has caught time and shaken it so that the period of great opulence, when Italian olives could not be had for love nor money and yoghurt and rice were part of the diet, seems oddly mixed with frost and famine and fields.

In Beckett's play for radio, *All That Fall*, Mr Rooney and his wife Maddy Rooney muse, with increasing hysteria, on the malady of the quotidian – work, housework, bills – as a mad wind blows around them and nature makes faint and frightening sounds. Suddenly, Mr Rooney says: Do you know, Maddy, sometimes one would think you were struggling with a dead language. After a while, Mrs Rooney replies: Well, you know, it will be dead in time, just like our own dear Gaelic, there is that to be said.

In *Trad*, Doherty plays with the conflict between a living speech and language as dead or deadening. Dialogue is a richly comic set of distorted echoes. Nothing is clear; most snatches of dialogue are desperately intended to be misunderstood. Words, like memory itself, will be dead in time, but for the purposes of the drama, they are only half dead, loudly threatening to expire.

In this production, the actors refuse to believe this. They play every word as full of meaning, ready to live forever. They demand that each other makes sense, and become immensely frustrated when words and slogans slip and fail, when cliché seems responsible for speech, and when memory is a sour trick played on us all. Their dilemma is all the more absurd for being completely unrecognised.

Trad takes its bearings from certain classics and crypto-classics of Irish Modernism – most notably Beckett's *Watt*, Flann O'Brien's *The Poor Mouth* and John Banville's *Birchwood*. The tone is rueful; the structure absurd. Ireland, its broken history, its mad martyrs, its interminable bad luck, its racism and its land-grabbers, becomes a comic metaphor for the plight of mankind. All you can do is make lists and then erase them, make sour comments in the margins, mix up many events and hector those around you. A nation becomes the same people saying exactly the same things in the same place, making no sense. I itch, therefore I am.

Work like this depends on echoes, is in urgent need for pricks to kick and hallowed voices to mock and undermine. Just as Beckett plays against all conventions of fiction and drama, until there is only voice, and Flann O'Brien mocks all forms of Irish discourse, and Banville plays with the Gothic style, Mark Doherty finds moments in the work of Synge and John B. Keane worthy of his sharp attention. But he is not interested in parody, more the thickening of the plot by allowing playful echoes into the recipe.

Directing such a play, and performing these roles, is to walk a very dangerous tightrope. Since this is not realism – there is no kitchen sink or hall door or natural timespan – then it would be easy to view it as merely absurd and play it for its strangeness, as an antidote to the work being done all around. These characters are not obviously credible; they remind us of people we know only in dreams or in vague flashes of memory. But just as Watt and his musings (or the universe of pure imagination of Flann O'Brien or pure voice of John Banville) become present, living for us by pure power of will mixed with magic, so too this quest, by a father and his son for some sign that the past and the future might connect, has a real power and presence.

The play does not depend on plot, or perfectly rounded characters. It depends instead on a peculiar energy, edgy, jerky, immensely funny, and fast and clever. In Mikel Murfi's production, this energy is mined for all it is worth, so the dark world of the father and his son, and their grave search, and Sal's musings on modernity, become a serious theatrical universe, convincing and engrossing, constantly surprising, full of astonishing verbal twists and turns, and also, most importantly, totally mad and absurd. To lure us gently in against our better judgment to a specially created artificial universe, where nothing makes sense, and render it real and true and compelling, is an important achievement for the writer, the director and the actors.

For the audience, it is a rare experience.

Colm Tóibín is a journalist, novelist and playwright.

The Bush Theatre

'What happens at The Bush today is at the very heart of tomorrow's theatre' (Sunday Times)

The Bush Theatre is a writers' theatre. We commission, develop and produce exclusively new plays. In addition to reading every script sent in and presenting eight new plays a year, we commission writers and provide dramaturgical support, script-reading services and bespoke development programmes.

Since its opening in April 1972, The Bush Theatre has grown to become a leading new writing venue, premiering the finest new writing talent and receiving over 100 awards. Bush plays have transferred to The West End and Broadway, toured throughout Britain, Europe, North America and Asia, and have been successfully adapted for film and television.

Artistic Director	**Mike Bradwell**
Executive Producer	**Fiona Clark**
Finance Manager	**Dave Smith**
Literary Manager	**Abigail Gonda**
Marketing Manager	**Nicki Marsh**
Production Manager	**Robert Holmes**
Theatre Administrator	**Nic Wass**
Chief Technician	**Sam Shortt**
Resident Stage Manager	**Ros Terry**
Acting Literary Assistant	**Will Kerley**
Administrative Assistant	**Lydia Fraser-Ward**
Box Office Supervisor	**Darren Elliott**
Box Office Assistants	**Rebecca Hartley, Gail MacLeod**
Front of House Duty Managers	**Kellie Batchelor, Adrian Christopher, Siobhan King-Spooner, Catherine Nix-Collins, Lois Tucker**
Duty Technicians	**Helen Spall, Tom White**
Associate Artists	**Tanya Burns, Es Devlin, Richard Jordan, Paul Miller**
Press Representation	**Alexandra Gammie** 020 7837 8333
Graphic Design	**Stem Design**
Sheila Lemon Writer in Residence	**Jennifer Farmer**
Pearson Writer in Residence	**Jack Thorne**

Be There At The Beginning

The Bush Theatre's international reputation of over thirty years is built on consistently producing the very best work to the very highest standard.

With your help this work can continue to flourish.

The Bush Theatre's Patron Scheme delivers an exciting range of opportunities for individual and corporate giving, offering a closer relationship with the theatre and a wide range of benefits from ticket offers to special events. Above all, it is an ideal way to acknowledge your support for one of the world's greatest new writing theatres.

To join, please pick up an information pack from the foyer, call 020 7602 3703 or email info@bushtheatre.co.uk

We would like to thank our current members and invite you to join them!

Rookies
Anonymous
Ross Anderson
Geraldine Caufield
Nina Drucker
John Gowers
Ms Sian Hansen
Lucy Heller
Mr G Hopkinson
Joyce Hytner, ACT IV
Casarotto Ramsay &
  Associates Ltd
Ray Miles
Mr & Mrs Malcolm Ogden
John & Jacqui Pearson
Clare Rich and Robert
  Marshall
Mark Roberts
Tracey Scoffield
Martin Shenfield
Alison Winter

Beautiful Things
Anonymous
Alan Brodie
Kate Brooke
David Brooks
Clive Butler
Matthew Byam Shaw
Jeremy Conway
Clyde Cooper
Mike Figgis
Vivien Goodwin
Sheila Hancock
David Hare
William Keeling
Laurie Marsh
Michael McCoy
Mr & Mrs A Radcliffe
John Reynolds
Barry Serjent
John & Tita Shakeshaft
Brian D Smith
Barrie & Roxanne Wilson

Glee Club
Anonymous
Jim Broadbent
Curtis Brown Group Ltd
Alan Rickman

Handful of Stars
Gianni Alen-Buckley

Lone Star
Princess of Darkness

Bronze Corporate Membership
Anonymous
Act Productions Ltd

Silver Corporate Membership
Anonymous
The Agency (London) Ltd
Oberon Books Ltd

Platinum Corporate Membership
Anonymous

The Bush Theatre, Shepherds Bush Green, London W12 8QD

The Alternative Theatre Company Ltd. (The Bush Theatre) is a Registered Charity number: 270080
Co. registration number 1221968
VAT no. 228 3168 73

www.bushtheatre.co.uk | 020 7610 4224

TRAD

First published in 2006 by Oberon Books Ltd
521 Caledonian Road, London N7 9RH
Tel: +44 (0) 20 7607 3637 / Fax: +44 (0) 20 7607 3629
e-mail: info@oberonbooks.com
www.oberonbooks.com

A catalogue record for this book is available from the British
Library.

ISBN: 978-1-84002-652-8

For G.P. and Granddad

Acknowledgements:

Sylvie;

Rose Cobbe;

Lynne Parker, Loughlin Deegan, Ali Curran
and everyone involved in 'Seeds';

Mikel, Frankie, Peter and David,
for turning *Trad* into a play;

Jim, and our musicians,
for lifting the play another notch;

Rose Parkinson and all at The Galway Arts Festival,
without whose faith and support
Trad would not have happened.

Author's Note

It is difficult for anyone reading *Trad* to imagine the effect of the music in our original (and currently ongoing) production. Back in 2003, when I had finished a draft, I approached Jim Doherty with some vague ideas about live music for the show. (Besides his credentials as a jazz pianist and composer, Jim has also written extensively for theatre.) Somehow, he took my inarticulate notions and created the original score for guitar and fiddle. It was exactly what I meant, and a lot more! It wasn't just complementary to the text; it gave our production another dimension, and helped turn it into a complete theatre show. I would ask anyone considering a production of *Trad* to check out this music. Please contact: jimdoherty@iolfree.ie

Characters

SON (or) THOMAS

DA

SAL

FATHER RICE

1. The House

Music: one minute intro.
Interior cottage.
DA is asleep. SON is standing. He has one arm.
Music ends.

SON: Da…? Da…? Da…? Da…? Da…? Da…? Da…?
Da…? Da…?

DA: What!

SON: I've a nice cup of tea for you.

DA: Tea…? Sure there was no tea!

SON: No da.

DA: Tea? Are you having me on?

SON: You're addled, da – I'll leave it for you there.

DA: Sure we didn't even have the water.

SON: No da.

DA: Did we?

SON: No da.

DA: Never mind the tea!

SON: I know, da…but there's a cup there for you now.

DA: Or cups… Where's me gansey?*

SON: Your what?

DA: Me gansey…! Are you Irish at all?

SON: I am da.

---

* 'gansey'; Gaelic, meaning: 'woolly jumper'.

DA: Well I don't see much evidence of it.

SON: You don't need it, da.

DA: I'll judge what I need thank you… Tea…!

SON: I was Irish last night.

DA: Were you boozing?

SON: I was.

DA: Good man!

SON: I sang a ballad, then fought a man.

DA: English?

SON: He was.

DA: Good man…! Tea…! And there wasn't a spud in the ground that year.

SON: What year, da?

DA: That year…! With the frost…and the rains…

SON: Aye.

DA: And we'd forgotten to plant any the previous year –

SON: Aye.

DA: Aye…with the frost, and the rains… If me great-grandmother –

SON: Me great-great-grandmother?

DA: If your great-great-grandmother hadn't got that award –

SON: We're off again!

DA: – for new fiction –

SON: Aye da!

DA: – for her autobiography – there wouldn't have been a – a –

SON: A crust on the table!

DA: Crusts? Are you having me on?

SON: No da.

DA: That year?

SON: Aye.

DA: Would you stop – a crust wouldn't have survived!

SON: No da.

DA: It would have been devoured!

SON: Aye!

DA: Stuck between two bits of bread and devoured... I'll tell you this – If me mother –

SON: Me grandmother?

DA: If your grandmother hadn't been the inter-county 'picking berries' champion, we'd never have eaten –

SON: Never have eaten.

DA: – we had blackberries for breakfast, loganberries for lunch and dinner, gooseberry tart for puddin' and raspberry feckin' treats with strawberry-berry tea...

SON: A hooer for the vitamin C.

DA: Hah...? Do you know what it's like? Living in a house full of people who smell of jam?

SON: I do not.

DA: You do not is right! The place was so full of wasps
– you couldn't – you couldn't –

SON: You couldn't swing a wasp!

DA: You could not… And if you swung one, sure, the others
would get fierce jealous, and you'd have to give them all
a go… If me father –

SON: Me grandfather?

DA: If your grandfather hadn't been the inter-county
'swinging striped insects' champion… Or so he claimed
anyway…

SON: A great man.

DA: A great man.

SON: A great man is right.

DA: A great man is right… And a fierce liar.

SON: He was.

DA: Aye… If he said he'd do something – he wouldn't.

SON: Aye… And if he said he wouldn't do something – he
would.

DA: Aye… And if he didn't – he'd say he had.

SON: Aye – then deny it.

DA: Aye… Passed away God bless him the following year
– during The Great Olive Crisis…

SON: With respect, da –

DA: Or so he claimed…

SON: With respect, da – I think that might have been the
Greeks, or somethin' off the wireless…

DA: The Great Olive Crisis – you'd be too young to
    remember that.

SON: Aye da.

DA: Couldn't get good olives for love nor money. Ohhh
    you'd get the Spanish ones alright, but what good is a
    Spanish olive to a palate that's used to the Italian ones...

   Pause.

   Where was I?

SON: Same place, da...

DA: The Great Olive Crisis – one of the worst disasters that
    decade.

   Pause.

SON: Worse than 1916?

DA: Hah...?

SON: 1916?

DA: Ah...! The oxygen ban! And nobody allowed to
    breathe on weekdays... Worse...! Nineteen hundred
    and sixteen...

   Pause.

SON: Wasps?

DA: Years, man! Years...!

   Pause.

   How many summers have you seen now?

SON: A hundred this year.

DA: A hundred... There's a fine age... A good even
    number... And me?

SON: You'd never tell us da.

DA: It'd be more than that, I suppose.

SON: It would, da, be definition…

DA: And me blood's gone bad, and me bones is nothin' but shells.

SON: Ah you've a year or two left in you yet.

DA: Years me arse – it's the minutes I'm counting. I thought I was gone last night… Oh Jesus…it's closing in on me…the whole thing… The end of the line…

SON: Are you feeling better with that?

DA: I am.

SON: You were dreaming.

DA: Was Calvey in?

SON: No da… Calvey's gone, da.

DA: Aye… I don't get addled you know.

SON: I know da.

DA: Just muddled.

SON: Muddled's grand.

DA: 'Addled' and I'd give a shite… 'Muddled' and you just have to work a bit harder… The end of the line is right… No men left…with blood relative to mine anyways…

Pause.

SON: I'm left…

DA: The end of the genes.

SON: I'm left da.

DA: Aye. And what good is that to anyone? What good is a bar with no booze?

SON: Can we not do this one again, please?

DA: What is it then only a room...? An empty room like this.

SON: Aye.

DA: Aye is right... No men left... A big empty room...with a man and a half in it.

SON: Aye da.

DA: Do you hear me?

SON: I do.

DA: A half a man... Have you nothing to say...? The end of the family... Hah? We put an end to all that. The end of the line.

SON: Aye da.

DA: Aye da...

SON: I might go for a rest.

DA: Go for a rest, so – don't stand up for yourself, like an Irishman would.

Pause.

A true Irish man... A full-blooded man... A full man!

SON: Aye!

DA: Aye...! Aye da! Aye da! Hah?

SON: Aye da.

DA: Aye da! No men left... All gone... Aye –

SON: Look will you not be saying that?

DA: Saying what?

SON: That!

DA: Well it's the truth, isn't it? Hah…?

SON: Yes!

DA: Well don't act all hurt then. If the truth hurts a man so much, then there's something wrong. Or I should say – if the truth hurts 'a half a man' so much, hah…? Nah – no response! Nothing to say, I suppose… End of the name…gone…'cause of one bad link…one little defected fella…or a half a one…a half a man –

SON: (*Exploding.*) I am not a half a man! Look at me! What do you see? Where do you see a half a man?

DA: And where's your wife, man?

SON: I never had a wife, da.

DA: I don't see her.

SON: Nor I da.

DA: And where's your son?

SON: I don't know where my son is. I don't know.

DA: Well then!

SON: He's somewhere!

Pause.

DA: What did you say…?

SON: Out there… He's somewhere…

DA: Who is…? Don't you lie to me.

SON: No da…

DA: So what are you saying he's somewhere? Who's somewhere? How is he out there?

SON: Because he is.

DA: Thomas…?

SON: So there…! I'm saying it, 'cause I've been forced into saying it… There was an incident… There was a girl.

DA: A girl?

SON: A girl!

DA: What sort of a girl?

SON: A girl, da – a girl! A human lady…! A girl from the village across.

Pause.

DA: Now just in case I'm not –

SON: You're hearing…! I had drink on me.

DA: Dear God and all His mystery… When?

SON: A while back.

DA: Sure that means nothing! Everything was a while back!

SON: Three moons after me birthday, da – me twenty-ninth birthday.

DA: So…?

SON: Aye.

DA: And…

Pause.

But…you know that's all I was hanging on for… Didn't you…? And her…? You know that was my reason? Hah…?

Pause.

Get me leg!

Pause.

SON: Hah?

DA: Get me leg!

SON: Ah da!

DA: Thank you!

SON: But… Where are you…?

DA: I'm waiting!

SON: Ah da!

DA: There's a child belonging to me wandering around out there for seventy years and I never met him. I've a trip left in me. The leg! Please…?

SON: Where is it, da?

DA: You're the one who does all the snoopin'! The dresser I think.

SON: Are you sure you…?

DA doesn't respond. SON begins searching.

DA: And hurry up! (*To himself.*) You're like an aul' one.

SON: (*Calling.*) When did you use it last, da…? Da…?

DA: What?

SON: (*Calling.*) Was it for the funeral?

DA: (*To himself.*) You know exactly when it was…

SON returns carrying a false limb, with a shoe on the end, and a hurley stick.

SON: Found it…! Shoe and all!

DA: Give us it here.

He tests it.

SON: She's stiff, da.

DA: She'll match well so…

DA begins to attach the leg.

SON: Aye… What…? Where…eh…? Da?

DA: (*Pointing under his bed.*) Give us one of them. I'll need me strength.

SON: Which?

DA: Them! Them!

The SON takes out an old, dusty carton.

SON: Ah da…! They're gone off!

DA: I'll tell you if they're off or not.

SON: Ah da!

He sticks in a finger and eats.

DA: Nothin' wrong with that! Except the price – a shillin' for that?

SON: Ah it's gone da!

DA: And the size of it? There's a Sassanach behind that shop.

SON: Is it not meant to be more – 'liquidy'?

DA stands, with his leg attached. He uses the hurley as a wealking stick

DA: Yoghurts is yoghurts…

He takes a few extremely slow steps towards the door.

Are you going to stand there all contrary, or are you comin'…?

SON: Ah da…!

Musical transition as they move outside very slowly. Jaunty in tone – twenty seconds.

2. The Journey Begins

Music ends.
Outside.
DA is doubled over, exhausted. SON leans against him.

SON: Will we head back, da…?

DA: We'll have a quick rest.

SON: Aye… How's the leg?

DA: Which one?

SON: The good one?

DA: Bad.

SON: Aye…

DA: Was it a lad?

SON: I think it was.

DA: I'd say it was too… That air's got fierce thin… And her? A child outside of marriage? Did she move, she did?

SON: I'm not certain, da.

DA: To England…to London… He might have grown up there…made some money…hah? Got in with the wrong crowd – married a Royal?

SON: Ah da!

DA: And us sittin' here not knowing we might be related to them feckin' Germans.

SON: Ah no da – I believe she stayed put.

DA: And how didn't I hear about it? A child born out of wedlock? There was few of them I didn't know about.

SON: They hide them things careful enough, da.

DA: It's better like that sometimes, hah? And not upsetting the whole community… And what name did you give him?

SON: I don't know da.

DA: You don't know?

Pause.

And what name did she have on her? The hooer?

SON: She wasn't a one of them da. All she was was a bit forward was all.

DA: What clan did she belong to is me question? It's important a man knows which are his cousins.

SON: I didn't get her family name, da…

DA: You didn't get her family name…? So the child had no name, and the mother had no family name.

SON: It was a while back da…!

DA: And her first name?

SON: 'Mary,' da.

DA: Mary...? Mary...! Isn't that great! There's a great help! Mary!

SON: We weren't on those sort of terms, da!

DA: Am I hearing this right? You knew her well enough to conceive a child with the hooer, but she wouldn't be so intimate as to give you her name?

SON: Ah da!

DA: Well aren't you some tulip.

SON: I was forced da. I was lead on. We didn't say two words to each other. She just – you know...gave me one of them stares...

DA: One of them stares?

SON: Aye.

DA: So – yous both stared, and lo – a child was born! And you who doesn't believe in miracles?

SON: Ah da!

DA: No – in me limited understanding of internals, Thomas, I never heard of a woman gettin' fertilized by a stare.

SON: No – it sort of – suggested we go round the back, and that she had something to show me.

DA: And she did, by the results...! Do you see the challenge we have in front of us now? There was a child – probably male, possibly female – born a number of years ago – we're not sure when – either in this country or elsewhere – to a strumpet named Mary – nothing more – just Mary. All we have for certain is – she had a powerful stare on her?

SON: Seventy da. That's for sure! It's a lad. And he'd have seventy years on him…

DA walks on ahead.

Da…?

DA: Follow me.

SON: Where are we going…? It's too far da! (*Calling.*) It's an hour to the village – on youngfellas' legs! They won't remember us! They'll lock us up, da!

DA: Do you want to find your son?

SON: I do.

DA: Good! 'Mary!' Does the train run still?

SON: She doesn't stop below, da.

DA: Does she not now! Good! Come on…

SON: Ah da…!

DA: We're takin' a trip!

Jaunty music accompanies them again as they take off – thirty seconds.
They negotiate obstacles, fences, ditches, etc.

3. The Field

Music ends.
DA and SON stop again

DA: This was owned by Old Coyle – and the orchard beyond – or so he used to claim –

SON: But you can't own –

DA: But of course as me father –

SON: Me grandfather?

DA: As your grandfather used to say – you can't own a tree... The Coyles... Great men indeed... 'Businessmen.' Done very, very, very, very, very well for themselves... They assimilated very well.

SON: Ah da!

DA: You know where they're from?

SON: Brits.

DA: Welshmen! I knew Old Coyle – arrived on the train at the harbour below – a pocket full of cash and not a manner in sight. But that's the English for you.

SON: You said Wales, da.

DA: An island is an island. Ask the foot-and-mouth... (*Screams.*) I'll not drink your soup, tourist.

SON: He's been here long enough, da.

DA: Long enough for what?

SON: I'm just sayin'!

DA: Rice has been here long enough – is it Irish?

SON: Ah da!

DA: Ah da nothin'... If they're not born and bred do you know what that makes them? Tourists! Plain and simple! And while the tourist is welcome to our postcards, he's not welcome to our land, and he's not welcome to a passport. Am I wrong?

SON: No da.

DA: No da…! Invaders! Makin' us something we aren't. Creatin' competition where it doesn't belong. That's the killer… What does that lead to only greed? Aye… You don't become Irish by hanging around in Ireland. It's to do with the genes. It's a way – an attitude. It's a pride thing… Tradition!

SON: Is it true Old Coyle was the ugliest man on record?

DA: He was. And some feat, with the competition…

SON: Bull-face Barrett…?

DA: Aye.

SON: Scaley Byrne…?

DA: Aye.

SON: Leaky-Noel McGrath…?

DA: Aye – uglier even than Monkfish and Pointy Cathleen McCall's kids… Come on!

They move again.

SON: Fine swimmers though… Do we have a plan, da?

DA: What are you like with your questions! My plan is to draw in air at the end of this sentence, and if I'm successful, I'll release it after, if I'm let…! Here's the plan – 'trust in God – '

SON: Ah da!

DA: ' – and you'll get your reward…!' In the meantime – we need apples.

Music over the following – twenty seconds.
DA attempts to climb a wall.

SON: Hah…?

DA: Apples…!

SON: Hah?

THOMAS helps his DA up onto the wall, and over.

4. The Orchard

Music ends.
They pick themselves up, and begin gathering apples.

DA: The ones going soft are the best… Aye – meself and
Calvey robbed this orchard every day for forty years…
me great, great friend.

SON: Me great-great-great-friend?

DA: Go away out of that – you didn't hardly know him.
From the moment the fruit appeared, to the last hangin'
apple in autumn – we stripped the place! Old Coyle, to
the day of his death never knew they were fruit-bearin'
trees! We told him an English was killed one time by a
small dog – and local trees bear no fruit with Sassanach
blood in the soil! Fact!

SON: Nice one, da!

DA: Aye…! Manus Calvey – the proudest Irish man this
land ever produced. You know his field?

SON: I do.

DA: A legend!

SON: Aye… Did he marry, da? Calvey?

DA: He did not, rest him.

SON: But he had a child and all?

DA: He had a child, aye – and he never saw him. Died before the creature was born…

SON: What did they make of that?

DA: It wasn't spoken of much – in public anyway… Worked himself to the bone he did, and then some. But Christ that field was magnificent…

SON: Did you eat them all?

DA: The apples? Some.

SON: And the rest?

DA: Let's say we prevented their consumption.

SON: By peltin' them?

DA: By peltin' them is right!

SON: We've a bagful da!

DA: Good man…

SON: Will we have one?

DA: We won't! Walk this way…

SON: What then…?

DA: If me geography's intact – the track is below – and beyond it – the cemetery?

SON: Ah da…! Are we pelting them at the train?

DA: You're a good lad!

SON: Ah da!

DA: You turned out grand! Come on!

Music – twenty seconds – as they move to the track.

5. The Train

The lads are sitting. DA is in deep thought.
Music ends.

DA: 'Whom…'

SON: Hah?

DA: 'Whom.'

SON: Whom?

DA: Aye… The English says that – instead of 'who'.

SON: Aye…

DA: It's dark enough, hah?

SON: We're not going to find him, da. And not sittin' here.

DA: We are going to find him, and if we don't find him we'll find the story, and the family goes on, and we'll rest in peace… Can you smell it?

SON: The salt?

DA: Prolongs the lungs… Would you want to be anywhere else? 'I would not,' says you, and who'd blame you.

Pause.

Thomas – have I discussed with you ever the signing over of the house?

SON: You did.

DA: That way, do you see, the taxman doesn't get a sniff.

SON: Several times.

DA: Aye – she's bought and paid for you see. All taken care of. That's the way to be, hah?

SON: Aye.

DA: Never owed a bank nor a lender nor landlord a bob in me life.

SON: Aye.

DA: Not a farthing.

SON: Aye.

DA: Is that the train? I think I hear something…?

SON: Does that make you happier than them who does?

DA: A free man, obliged to nobody.

Pause.
Train – suggested by rhythmic music – in the distance.
Music runs through the scene, gradually gaining momentum
– two minutes.

SON: And what did you do with it?

DA: Hah?

SON: Why did you never leave? And seek your fortune?

DA: Sure what's money only tickets to trouble.

SON: I don't mean money, da.

DA: There's nothin' gives a man a smell of himself like a few bob more than he's due.

SON: Your fortune, though – your luck?

DA: Sure you make your bed. I chose here.

SON: You never left the country.

DA: Correct! I did not…! The Chair Lavelle never left his house!

SON: Ah da!

DA: Am I wrong? Unless you have information wasn't available to the rest of us?

SON: He wasn't right, da!

DA: Never left his house!

SON: His mind wasn't right, da!

DA: And when did you become a doctor all of a sudden?

SON: Ahhhh...! It was well known!

Music gains momentum.

DA: Is this some class of an interrogation...? And if you're so concerned about travelling the world and makin' a fortune, what are you sittin' here for?

SON: I did leave.

DA: Humorin' simple eejits like me?

SON: Did you forget?

DA: Aye – and you came back quick enough.

SON: Don't push me no more, da!

DA: Aye...tail between the legs!

SON: You know very well why I came back.

DA: And who'd blame you... Who'd want to be part of that?

SON: Are you hearin' anything at all?

DA: Shush...! Listen! I think she's comin'.

DA stands, listening.

I think she's comin'...!

SON: Aye… She's comin' da!

Music gains momentum – train approaches.

DA: I'm here! I'm here! Positions…!

SON: I'll lob them!

DA: Positions…! Closing batsman!

SON: Ready…!

The arrival of the train is represented by rhythmical music, and lighting effect…

DA: Keep them comin'!

With each 'pull!' SON lobs an apple – DA pelts them at the train with the hurley.

And… Pull…! Pull…! Pull…! Pull…! Pull…! Pull…!

The train (music) goes off into the distance. The lads are exhausted but thrilled.

Missed the second coach…!

SON: You done well, da…!

DA: Happy enough…! Right…! We have to keep moving.

SON: Ah da!

DA: Come on!

SON: Come on where? Are we going to the graveyard?

DA: 'Cemetery.'

SON: But…?

DA moves on.

There'll be nobody there.

DA: There'll be plenty there! It's who isn't there we're interested in! And that's why we're goin' – see who's left…! Narrow the field down a bit!

SON: You'll get sad, da.

DA: I've done me grieving. Come on!

Train music reprise – twenty seconds.
THOMAS follows, with difficulty, as usual.

6. The Graveyard

Music ends.
The lads take in the atmosphere in silence.

DA: What do you feel?

SON: What do you mean?

DA: What do you feel?

SON: How do I feel?

DA: No.

SON: What then…? What do you feel?

DA: I feel the history.

SON: Oh… Me and all…

They look at all the gravestones.

DA: And it makes me sad… So many of the greats… You won't put me in the ground, will you?

SON: Ah da!

DA: I have to be sure.

SON: And I'm always telling you!

DA: Good man!

Pause.

SON: Da...?

DA: What?

SON: I was just thinkin' – just while we're here –

DA: No.

SON: – that we might –

DA: I said no!

SON: No da... You're probably right... We could leave some flowers for her?

DA: No.

SON: Aye...

DA: Look't! Legend number one! Baits!

SON: Hah?

DA: Baits Lavelle – one of the finest!

SON: Boatmen!

DA: Aye...! Knew the preferred supper of every fish in the ocean, and what time of day they dined.

DA and SON pause again, looking around the theatre.

Look at them all...

SON: Hundreds of them...

DA: And most of them younger than us.

SON: Most of them... (*Another grave.*) Mangan?

DA: The only wake I ever attended that stretched into a
    third week. Legend!

SON: What got him? Was it the booze?

DA: It was not!

SON: No!

DA: There was them who said it was –

SON: And it wasn't?

DA: It was not – no... No... Though I suppose it was really!

SON: I have him now!

DA: Stumbling along the coast road with six days and
    nights of porter inside of him, didn't he urinate so
    heavily against the lighthouse wall –

SON: It came down on him!

DA: Aye...

They look at various graves.

The Calveys! Full house! Except for Manus of course...
Buried above in the field... Look't! John Patton! Seanie!
Legend...! Stamps O'Hagan...! She would have had
your little secret! Took her job very serious... Read
every letter that ever went through the post office!

SON: They're all gone, da.

DA: So they said anyway.

SON: That's it so...

THOMAS moves to leave.

DA: Where do you think you're going?

SON: Hah…? Home!

DA: Good…! Very good! And would you like me to pass on a message to the boy?

SON: Ah da!

DA: 'I'm sorry your daddy couldn't come – '

SON: It's getting dark!

DA: 'It's just he always preferred to half do things than do them proper.'

SON: Everybody's gone, da.

DA: Have faith!

SON: Faith…? This is real, da.

DA: And that's your problem. You never believed in anything in your life.

SON: Look around you…? Gone! They're all gone… Sweeney – gone…! Meagher – gone…! Patton. Scully. They're gone, da. It's useless. We're searchin' for nothing. Look at us! We'll cover ten furlongs a day – and that with a good tail wind – and whatever the feck his name is could be in Melbourne feckin' Australia!

A noise off – someone is approaching.

DA: Whisht a sec!

SON: Hah?

Muttering is heard from the shadows.

DA: Shush…! Somebody's comin'…!

SON: Who's comin'?

DA: Shush! It's probably a son.

SAL enters, slowly, from the shadows.

SON: A son of who, da?

DA: Coyle – Brits! Quick…! Give us a stone!

SON: Ah da!

DA and SON scramble into position, ready for attack.

DA: More stones – quick!

SON: It's the cemetery, da!

DA: Natural…! Nice and natural.

SAL: Is that Father? Father…? I've been waiting on you, Father.

DA: Still a minute.

SAL: 'Tis me – Sal… I'm fadin', Father.

DA: Who's there…? Oh Jesus and all the saints!

SAL: Father?

DA: Sal…! Sal! 'Tis not the priest, love! 'Tis meself and Thomas.

SAL: Is Father Rice with ye?

DA and SON present themselves.

DA: From the top house above, Sal…? We used to come in the shop love? One or both of us…? Goin' back a bit now.

SAL: I need the priest… I need his blessing.

DA: Do you recall us, Sal?

Pause.

SAL: The top house…? One of ye was the other one's father.

DA: Aye! That's meself, love!

SAL: There was a girl?

DA: There was no girl, Sal.

SON: There was me ma, Sal!

SAL: Lilly!

DA: Aye.

SAL: Lord rest her a beautiful girl.

DA: The most beautiful.

SON: You remember her?

SAL: And taken previous.

DA: Aye.

SAL: The lucky ones go quick and at their time… I was pretty too… Do you feel it? The energy, hah…?

DA: We feel somethin', Sal.

SAL: Aye… Maybe that's the Holy Spirit they taught us.

DA: Aye.

SAL: We'll know soon enough, please God.

DA: Aye.

SAL: Aye is right… Or maybe not …

SAL makes her way to her husband's grave.

DA: Are you not freezing love…?

SAL: Aye! It gets you in the end, hah? You're born warm…

DA: You're visiting himself, Sal…?

SAL: They get no exercise so they do the weights.

Pause.

DA: Who's that, love?

SAL: Aye… They sit in front of the computers all day, then do the weights in the night-time – in the gymnasium.

DA: Is that right?

SAL: Aye… They have the childer in the Montessori – don't even talk to them. Put them in front of the television, stick the breakfast in them, send them off, pick them up when the light is gone, shovel food into them, and put them back in the bed again. Is it any wonder they can't talk to each other anymore?

DA: It is not.

SAL: Only by the wireless telephone.

DA: Is that right?

SAL: We looked after each other – made sure we were never wanting.

DA: Aye.

SAL: 'Tis all money now, hah?

DA: That's it!

SAL: Hah?

DA: Aye…

SON: Sal…? Could we ask you a question? Goin' back a bit now, but we're trying to track down the whereabouts of a certain person.

SAL: And what name do they have on them?

SON: Well this is it you see – we don't know for certain. We believe it's a lad –

DA: Might resemble young Thomas here by all accounts, only a younger version.

SAL: They give them guns in America.

DA: Who's that, love?

SAL: Before they're out of nappies – one of Lavelle's was shot there in Chicago.

DA: Is that right?

SAL: He was. Twice – in the one day. Coming out of the hospital, a bandage round his head, and didn't the doctor shoot him.

DA: There's a thing, hah?

SAL: Ah it's gone wrong.

DA: Gone wrong is right, Sal!

SAL: Am I wrong?

SON: Sal – I'll tell you what we know of this fella, and you might be able to shed some light on it for us.

SAL: And how many years does he have on him?

SON: Seventy.

DA: Born local, aye – seventy years back.

SAL: Seventy? There's few enough of them... Is it Pots? Nets Lavelle's lad? He'd be that.

SON: It's not one of the Lavelles, Sal, no.

SAL: There's Shoulders…? He'd be seventy-four, if not seventy-six. The Guinea McGrath?

SON: It's not the Guinea, Sal.

SAL: Well then I can't assist you… Did you talk to Rice?

SON: Father Rice?

SAL: Below at the harbour? He'd have all the records.

DA: He would, I suppose.

SAL: Is it Calvey's son you're looking for? Across on the island?

DA: It's not him, Sal.

SAL: You were tight – you and Calvey.

DA: Wasn't I his loyal and constant companion – in all but vows!

SAL: Aye… I was pretty, hah?

Pause.

They love the photographs.

DA: Who's that Sal?

SAL: The Japanese.

DA: They do and all!

SAL: Don't belong here, hah?

DA: Different genes.

SAL: Hah?

DA: Don't know Sal.

SAL: And the blacks?

DA: Aye.

SAL: You wouldn't know if you were in Ireland or feckin'
Nairobi... Hah? With their this and their that and their
coughing and their spitting.

DA: Aye... Listen we'll take our leave of you Sal. I should
be getting this fella home – it's past his bedtime... You'll
be alright, love?

SAL: I'll go 'til I stop, I suppose...

SAL begins her exit.

DA: We'll see you, Sal.

SAL: Aye... If Your Man intends it.

DA: Aye... God bless you, love.

SAL: You'll tell him to say a prayer for me? Rice?

DA: We will Sal...We'll do that... Slán...*

SON: Goodbye, Sal.

She exits.
Music begins – two minutes – a slow ballad – over the
following scene.

SON: I have to sit a sec, da.

DA: Aye...

SON: We'll rest and then get back.

DA: Aye... She's addled, Sal, hah?

SON: She's ready to go, da.

DA: No one decides that only Himself, hah...? Hah?

* 'Slán'; Gaelic, meaning: 'goodbye'.

SON: Aye da…

THOMAS nods off over the following. DA is exhausted also.

DA: Aye da… She has her faith, you see… She has her direction, hah…? 'Show me the way,' says the fella to Himself up there…when He was down here… 'I am the shepherd,' says Your Man… 'Trust in Me…and you'll never be wantin'.' Hah…? Aye… Aye is right…

7. Ma

Music continues under the following scene.
DA nods off also.
(We do not see the woman in this scene.)
Lighting change as DA slowly wakes. SON remains asleep.
DA stares ahead – he 'sees' his wife. He stands slowly.
He reaches out, taking her hand.
He kisses her gently, places her head by his, and they dance cheek to cheek to the music. DA moves fluidly and dances well – this is him as a younger man.
For a few moments they dance together to the music.
The woman then begins to move away.
DA stops, and stands in the centre, watching her slowly go.
He is left standing alone, without his stick.
The music ends.
SON wakes.

SON: Da…? Da…? Da…? Da –

DA: What…?

SON: Are you alright, da?

DA: I am.

SON: Are you awake?

DA: I don't know… I don't know….

SON: I had a dream!

DA: Good man…

SON: Aye… I think he might be droppin' into the house!

DA: Hah…? Who might be droppin' in?

SON: Himself – your man! Whatever his name is!

DA: Your son?

SON: Your grandson! Do you want your stick, da…?

DA: I do…I suppose… So he might be payin' us a visit, hah?

SON: Aye!

DA: And it hasn't occurred to him this last seventy years,
    but you think today might be the day?

SON: Aye… Assuming he's alive and all!

DA: Assuming he's alive, and in the country!

SON: Aye…! And that he knows who – who his father is.

DA: Aye.

SON: And where we live, like.

DA: Aye.

SON: Aye.

DA: Aye…

SON: It's slim, like…

DA: 'Tis…

SON: You don't give up though… Isn't that it, da?

DA: Aye…

SON: Are you tired?

DA: Most of me is – some less so.

SON: The legs?

DA: Not great, and not great at all.

SON: You'll sleep tonight… Is the bell working? Above at the house?

Pause.

DA: We're not going back.

SON: Hah…?

DA: No!

SON: Ah da…!

DA: No!

SON: We're gettin' further and further away.

DA: From what…?

SON: They're all gone da.

DA: It's not in the blood to give up. It's not Irish.

SON: What has Irish to do with anything?

DA: It's not in the genes.

SON: And what's the genes, da?

DA: Isn't it everything I'm telling you!

SON: Tell me what the genes is please!

DA: You don't give up!

SON: Tell me!

DA: It's not in our tradition!

SON: (*Exploding.*) Ahhhhhhhhh...! What is it that you
     want...? Da...? What is this tradition thing that
     gives you all your energy? Hah...? Your great-great-
     grandchildren telling the same stories that you're telling
     me now? And have told me all my life? Is that it? Is
     that what you want? Is that what tradition is? Everyone
     standing still and facin' backwards? And for their
     children to remember Manus Calvey with the same
     passion as you? 'Cause it won't happen, da. It can't
     happen. And that's it...! And that's the way it is. And
     I'm sorry.

DA: You missed my point.

SON: No I didn't miss your point...! I know your point very
     well. Your point has been driven home to me very well
     this hundred years. But I have to say me piece as well...
     Is it thanks to Manus Calvey and Scaley Byrne that
     there's men on the moon, and wireless telephones? No
     da...! And of course they're legends, but, like – there's
     a million, or a hundred million... feckin...like... You
     add yourself into the mix, whether you're a – you're...
     And let go... And the whole thing moves on... And...
     So there!

Pause. THOMAS is exhausted.

DA: Are you finished...?

SON: Yes.

Pause.

DA: There's a performance, hah...?

SON: I'm tired.

DA: Aye… Aye… We'll stop… It's better… We'll give up…
    It's easier that way…

SON: Ah da!

DA: Are you giving up or are you not…?

SON: No, da.

DA: Good… Good man!

SON: But we don't even know if the lad –

DA: We're goin' to Rice.

SON: The priest?

DA: Aye… He'll have the records of all them born in the
    parish.

SON: Will he though?

DA: Sal said it.

SON: I don't like him, da.

DA: Have faith.

SON: I don't trust him.

DA: You don't give up…!

SON: Aye da…!

*Ballad – twenty seconds – resumes, and accompanies them
onwards.*
They begin walking again.

8. Onwards

The lads are walking.
Music ends.

SON: I'm not calling an equal of mine 'Father'. Hah?

DA: Well that's the way it's done.

SON: A man who believes he's chosen? Would you not worry for a fella like that? And chosen by who? Some lad in his head? You need some imagination to settle on that, hah?

DA: And what harm has it caused you?

SON: Plenty of harm thank you! Sure if it wasn't the pressure them feckers put us under with their telling us what to be doing with our seeds... We might be surrounded by a family of fightin' lads, hah?

DA: You've some tongue on you.

SON: And what about Nets Lavelle...? And him a hero of yours? Didn't he scatter himself generously over every continent?

DA: Aye – wherever the fish lead him.

SON: And what harm? Sure that man could land in any port in any hemisphere north or south, in the full certainty that half the inhabitants would know him as 'da'. Was he bad?

DA: He wasn't.

SON: Well according to them feckers he was!

DA: Less of the 'feckers'!

SON: Just a man – who'd fall in love easier than most.

DA: That's what they teach us, so that's how it is. Patrick 'Nets' Lavelle... Do you know how many he had?

SON: Women? Or how many children?

DA: Same difference.

SON: There was versions, da.

DA: Do want the story? Or have you nothing you can learn anymore?

SON: Sure who did the story come from only himself?

Pause.

DA: And a man-to-man question – did you not – you know – get a flavour for it?

SON: Hah?

DA: You know – did you not...? Did you enjoy your time with the lady?

SON: It was grand, yeah.

DA: So did you not get a taste for more?

SON: The opportunities were rare, da.

DA: I'll give you that.

SON: Plus...

DA: And what?

SON: Ah...just – what Your Man said, and all...

DA: What did He say?

SON: Ah I don't know the wording exactly – but along the lines of getting married first, and love and all that, and not doing a Nets Lavelle on the community.

They stop for a rest.

DA: (*Breathing in deeply.*) Can you smell that…!

SON: Salt…!

DA: Aye… Prolongs the lungs! That's if you believe the medics anyway.

Pause.

And was there a session on?

SON: Hah?

DA: The Harbour?

SON: Hah?

DA: Below in the bar? Last night?

SON: Oh…!

DA: Was there?

SON: A session? Yes. There was.

DA: Did you join it?

Pause.

SON: (*Referring to his lack of arm.*) To be honest, da – I find the bowing troublesome ever since.

DA: Ah would you don't be exaggerating your woes.

SON: I'm not, da.

DA: You're Irish!

SON: And proud of it!

DA: Well where's the passion, man? 'Once a fiddler – '

SON: 'Always – ' I know da, but it's inconvenient still.

DA: Sure didn't Legs McMahon lose a toe on his left foot plus everything above the navel?

SON: So they say, da.

DA: And so it was. And did it stop him on the squeeze-box?

SON: I believe it didn't.

DA: You believe right. He won the feis not three days later.

SON: I suppose what you lack in technique –

DA: Passion, man! Passion!

SON: Legs and the aeroplane…

DA: Aye… Below in the bay…

SON: Experience can be a cruel teacher.

DA: Aye… Call it impatience –

SON: Enthusiasm?

DA: The exuberance of youth –

SON: A shortage of schooling?

DA: Never-ever-ever – stop the propeller of a moving aircraft from without…

SON: I'll bet he didn't try that one again!

DA: Well – that's the thing you see –

SON: Ah no!

DA: Ah yeah!

SON: Ah da!

DA: Aye...! Old Massey said it was the smallest coffin he ever had to build... That's the house below! Last stop!

Music – twenty seconds.
The lads set off again, down towards the harbour.

9. The Journey Continues

DA and SON pause to rest. They have little energy left.
Music ends.

SON: Have you strength, da?

DA: Enough...

He sits.

SON: Aye... How's the leg?

DA: Are you afraid of dying Tom?

SON: I am.

DA: So am I.

SON: Aye... And living...

DA: And do you know what it is has us that way? There was a time forty or fifty years ago I'd go to sleep at night full of confidence of waking up the following day –

SON: It's them, da! I'm telling you!

DA: Hah?

SON: The priests...

DA: Maybe it is.

SON: I never quite could communicate with them lads. I can honestly say I never relaxed in the company of one of them fellas... I don't like them, da.

DA: There's good and there's bad...

SON: And how's a man who never held a book supposed to get his head around all that?

DA: That's the mystery.

SON: The son of a virgin?

DA: So they say...

SON: And how is it we have all the details of it so perfect?

DA: The lads wrote it down.

SON: And how is it we lost years and decades since – and no one knows where they went – but the lads were able to chronicle every bowel movement That Fella had?

DA: Look't... You're not supposed to understand all the details of it...

THOMAS sits with his DA.

Even fellas with forty letters after them and fifty books on the subject have trouble gettin' their heads around it all... It's a young man's nature, I suppose, to ask too many questions. I would have been the same...

Pause.

Why didn't you tell us, Thomas?

SON: I don't know, da.

DA: Didn't you know all I ever wanted was for the family to carry on?

SON: It was wrong what I done...what happened. I didn't want – ah... You always expected high things of me da. You taught me to do right by people, and not be, you know – and you're a difficult – or I always found it hard to – to face up to you and – I couldn't, after what happened – 'cause of the feeling I'd be letting you down, 'cause of your pride, and all that.

DA: My pride?

SON: Aye... And I'm not saying it was your... Just that the circumstances and all that, and I didn't feel it was best to tell you, and that you'd be disappointed and all.

DA: Am I some kind of monster that you can't talk to me?

SON: No da.

DA: Were you afraid of me?

SON: No da. But I suppose I was a bit.

DA: You were then.

SON: Aye! But afraid isn't the word. I don't know what the word is now, but – that it's easier to agree with people than disagree sometimes. It's to do with the blood I suppose, and keeping it cool.

They reach the entrance to the priest's house.

DA: Good man...

SON: Will he be up, da?

DA: I see a light... After you, son.

SON: You go ahead, da.

DA: Go on ahead yourself.

SON: I'm here!

DA: Would you don't be behind me for once!

SON: We're not stayin'!

10. Father Rice

DA: Best behaviour!

SON: You can talk to him – I'm not talking to him.

DA: We needn't give him the particulars – just say it's a friend or a cousin we're lookin' for!

SON: I know, da...

DA hammers on the door with his stick.

DA: (*Calling.*) Father Rice...?

SON: We're not stayin', da!

DA: We'll be in and out.

RICE: (*Off.*) Who is it...?

DA: Tell him.

SON: It's Thomas, Father Rice... From the top house beyond... I've me da with me... We wanted to ask you a question or two, Father?

RICE: (*Off.*) Hah...?

SON: We'll not waste your time Father – it's just we're trying to track down the whereabouts of a certain fella!

DA: A cousin of ours!

RICE: (*Off.*) Hah?

DA: Can we come in, Father?

Door swings open. FATHER RICE appears.

RICE: Hah...? Is there two of ye, there is?

SON: There is.

RICE: Hah?

SON: There is.

RICE: Hah? One of ye's the other one's father?

DA: That's meself, Father.

RICE: Yourself? Is it...? Oh aye – I have you now... You'd be contemporaneous or thereabouts with meself, hah?

DA: I am, Father Rice.

RICE: I have you now.

DA: And are you still in operation down below, Father?

RICE: I am.

DA: You're lookin' well with it.

RICE: Hah?

DA: You're lookin' well!

RICE: Me blood's gone bad and me bones is nothin' but shells... But sure you keep goin', says you... And who'd replace me? Says you?

SON: Father –

RICE: I haven't seen ye lately?

DA: We don't get around too easily this weather.

RICE: Hah?

SON: We just wanted to ask you a quick question Father – about a certain man, and if you recall him. Going back a few years.

DA: You'd be doing us a great service, Father!

RICE: Come in so…

They enter the priest's house.

You'll have a taste?

SON: We won't, Father.

RICE: Hah? A small one?

SON: Father Rice, we'll not waste your time. We're lookin'
for a fella – not even sure if he lives local these days
– an old cousin of ours.

RICE: Oh aye?

DA: A distant relation.

RICE: And what name has he on him?

SON: We've never actually met him Father, so we don't
have his name. All we know is that he was born this
month or thereabouts, seventy years ago.

RICE: Hah? And what do you want from me?

DA: Old Sal said –

SON: We thought you might have a record of them
christened around the parish?

RICE: I'll have that for you easy enough… You were above
in the graveyard?

DA: We were, Father.

RICE: Hah? If you met herself you were…

*He blows dust from an old book, and opens it. DA and SON
sit.*

DA: Buck up.

SON: Ah da!

RICE: Now… Fellas-born – seventy years you say – on this day or thereabouts… There wasn't many… You'll have a taste?

SON: We won't…! Thank you…Father.

RICE: Suit yourselves… Now… (*Reading.*) Lavelle – Patrick, or 'Pots' as he's known – born this month seventy years ago, to Nets and Mags Lavelle –

DA: No – we know Pots, Father. It's not him.

RICE: It's not him? Boatmen – the Lavelles.

DA: Aye…

RICE: (*With disdain.*) Fishermen…

SON: Aye Father. It's not him.

RICE: Not him… Always fishin' they were… Some messers…! Let's see now – any other – childer… (*Reading.*) McGrath – Patrick, 'the Guinea' – there's one! The Guinea McGrath – born to Cait and Hens McGrath –

SON: Not him, no.

RICE: And how do ye know it's not him?

DA: We don't reckon it's him, Father –

RICE: Hah…? Ye are askin' me to find a fella and you don't even know what name he has on him, yet ye are certain the names I'm readin' are not the lad in question?

SON: Is there more, Father?

RICE: Hah…? The only other fella – 'twas a lad, aye?

SON: It was, Father.

RICE: (*He looks at the book again.*) The only other fella – born this month – seventy years ago – and the name on him – 'Calvey'.

DA: Manus Calvey's young fella!

RICE: Aye...

DA: That's what we were thinking.

THOMAS stands.

RICE: Well that's all I can do for ye... You were thick, yourself and Calvey?

DA: His loyal and constant companion!

RICE: In all but vows, says you!

DA: Aye!

RICE: Hah?

SON: Father Rice...? Is it in the records...what name did he give to his son?

RICE: Who? Calvey...? He gave no name to his son – wasn't he dead before the lad arrived!

DA: Aye.

RICE: God rest him...! There wasn't a man north south or east of here worked like Calvey.

SON: And... So what name did she give him – the mother?

DA: Nobody like him!

RICE: There was not...! I'll have that for you now... 'Thomas' the child's name was... 'Thomas Calvey'.

DA: A great man, Manus.

RICE: A great, great man.

DA: And a worker!

RICE: Hah?

DA: A worker!

RICE: Ah would you stop! The hardest workin' man the land ever knew.

SON: (*Pushing further.*) And can I ask you Father – who was the mother? I never heard of Calvey having a wife, or a lady friend of any description.

RICE: It was a miracle, you could say. The only one I ever witnessed.

DA: A gift from God.

RICE: Is right…!

SON: What – miracle…?

RICE: Well the story, as I remember it, went way back…

He invites THOMAS to sit.

Manus had a field, which was in the family for years. His great-great-grandfather, an inter-county 'tending fields' semi-finalist, had it originally, and gave it to Manus on the first anniversary of his conception. Manus – only three moons old – decided there and then it would be the finest field the village ever knew, even if it killed him –

DA: Which it did!

RICE: Aye! Well he spent the next fifty years tillin', ploughin', harvestin', tillin' –

DA: Diggin' –

RICE: Rakin', diggin' and tillin' that feckin' field. He'd start at six o'clock in the morning and labour solidly for twenty-four hours – and the same the next day.

DA: Aye – only on a Sunday would he take a rest.

RICE: Aye – and even that was in the field!

DA: Didn't I see it!

RICE: Aye – he'd lie on a wet patch of grass shaped like a wet green bed, and thank God for his field and for his health, which was declining rapidly. Then he'd punish himself for resting by diggin' the field again –

DA: Using only a shovel –

RICE: A shovel? A shovel the size of a spoon!

DA: Aye!

RICE: My God he worked. Sure his skin was like leather –

DA: His skin was like leather – but leather you couldn't see, so worn was it!

RICE: Aye…! And so it was, 'til late one summer's night, only a week after losing a leg in a harvester, disaster struck! Didn't he wear out his other leg. But did that stop him? Would you stop it did not stop him! It drove him on even harder, 'til his hands became stumps and his arms became his shoulders. He manœuvred himself around the field using only the lids of his eyes, and tilled using a tiny plough strapped to his tongue… Ahhh – he knew the work was damaging his health – but that only encouraged him.

DA: You get out of this life what you put into it!

RICE: Then late that autumn, the inevitable happened –

DA: Winter!

RICE: Aye! And a particular bastard it was. Manus's head became loose, and he could plough no more. He would leave his beloved field to the son he was less likely to have every hour. As the moon rose that evening, he dug himself a grave – it's not recorded how – and with his last remaining tooth, engraved himself a headstone. It's still there to this day – 'Manus Calvey – sixty – dead – due to erosion.' He rolled into the grave, and without a word of complaint, passed away peacefully, the following autumn.

Silence.

SON: And his son, Father?

RICE: Hah?

SON: His son…? How was it he came to have a boy?

RICE: Ah a fine lad and still with us across on the island.

SON: But how did it happen?

RICE: Aren't I coming to it, child…! Now there's them who believe – and there's them who doesn't believe – and them who look for proof of God's work before them. And this surely was it beyond doubt.

DA: A miracle?

RICE: Hadn't Manus, towards the end of his days, spilled his own personal seed several times, inadvertently, while rolling limbless around the field. And by the grace of God, mixed with a strange game the local girls play, didn't Máire Ni Suilabháin find herself heavy with the fruits of Manus's labour.

71

DA: A gift from God!

RICE: The greatest gift of them all…! And so a son was born, and Thomas Calvey his name – a fine Irish lad with a leathery hide, a love of the land in his blood, and a powerful stare on him… And he's still there today, across on the island, and a family of strappin' lads around him.

SON: Máire Ni Suilabháin!

RICE: Aye. Passed away a while, rest her.

DA: Hah…?

SON: Mary!

DA: Mary…?

RICE: Máire!

SON: Máire!

DA: Mary…? (*A moment.*) Mother – of – God!

RICE: And all His mystery.

SON: And all His mystery…!

DA: (*Stunned.*) All His mystery is right.

RICE: You'll have a drink now? I've a fierce drought on me throat.

Pause. DA remains stunned. THOMAS watches.

SON: We won't, Father.

RICE: Hah?

DA: No…

SON: But thank you, Father. We'll keep going.

DA: Aye.

RICE: And have I shed some light on it for ye?

DA: Yes…

SON: You have, Father.

RICE: Hah? Will you be gracing us one of these Sundays?

SON: If Your Man intends it, Father, we might… Thank you.

RICE: Aye… Please God says you!

DA: Yes.…

RICE: Please God… Hah?

> *FATHER RICE retreats to his house.*
> *Music begins, and continues into the next scene.*
> *Melancholy ballad – impression of the sea – waves.*

11. The Harbour

DA and SON stare out at the sea

DA: (*Breathing in and out deeply.*) She's high tonight…

SON: It's beautiful…!

DA: Full tide, hah…? The moon does that…for some reason…

SON: I have a son, da!

DA: Pulls her in and out.

SON: Just over there…! Do you hear me, da? I've a son!

DA: What do you want? A feckin' medal?

SON: 'Thomas!' Me name and all!

DA: Do you hear it...?

SON: Are we headin' across, da?

DA: I miss that somethin' terrible...

SON: The sea?

DA: And the salt...and the music...and the spray...and the gulls...and the wind...and the thrill... And you become a part of it –

THOMAS takes a rope, and pulls in a boat.

SON: Help us here, da!

DA: A living, moving, changing, frightening, exhilarating, beautiful thing... And no one can control it. And no one can own –

SON: Are we writing poems or feckin' a boat, da?

DA: I'm here! I'm here!

SON: I know thou shouldn't steal and all but –

DA: We'll borrow her just – no sin in that. You can bring her back tomorrow.

SON: Are you up to it, da?

DA: Hop down there and undo that rope.

SON: I'm a wreck!

DA: 'I'm a wreck!' You'll be tired in a minute alright...

SON: It's been a day, hah...!

THOMAS climbs carefully into the boat.

DA: Tired! And when have you ever been tired? Didn't myself and Manus transfer a mountain over sixty furlongs once?

SON: You did, da!

DA: And for what?

SON: Was it for mischief?

DA: It was not for mischief.

SON: Was it in defiance of an Englishman?

DA: It was not! It was blocking the sun. Plain and simple. So whisht with your complaining and help me on board.

DA climbs into the boat.

They left the oars for us and all! One each I suppose.

They begin to row.

DA: How's the arm?

SON: Which one?

DA: The good one?

SON: Grand!

DA: Me great-great-great-great-grandmother –

SON: Me great-great-great-great-great-grandmother?

DA: Aye – there's a woman who could swallow a drink.

SON: I've heard that.

DA: And I've witnessed it. An Englishman –

SON: 'Smedley'!

DA: – named Smedley – took a shine to her one time –

SON: Asks her out for a jar!

DA: And Smedley, not realising he had his eye on an inter-county 'holding booze' finalist, asks her out for a jar.

SON: Very unwise!

DA: 'Will you pay?' says she.

SON: 'I will' says he!

DA: I'm telling it… 'I will,' says he, and out they go.
It comes to midnight, he's slouched at the counter mumbling some rubbish about the Queen's extraordinary something, and she hasn't even knocked the edges off her thirst yet. 'Same again Joe,' says she, cool as you like, to – to – what's his name –

SON: Joe?

DA: To Joe – 'but mine's a large one if you please!' Another hour passes, and Smedley is white in the face and lying on the ground, reminiscing about chutney and garden fêtes – 'Joe?' says the great-great-great-great-grandmother –

SON: The great-great-great-?

DA: Are you going to keep interrupting?

SON: Sorry da.

DA: Me rhythm's upset now… So anyways, she says…to – what's his name at the bar –

SON: Joe…? Sorry!

Pause.

Go on da?

DA: Ahhh…sure you know it.

SON: I don't… I don't remember it, da…! How long did she go for? Come on da…! She could have drank for Ireland, couldn't she?

DA: She could.

Pause. DA stares at the water.

SON: And what happened in the end…? Didn't she drink for three days?

DA: Aye…

SON: Costing the booze-poisoned prod…?

DA: Costing the booze-poisoned prod…

SON: The grand total…?

DA: Aye…

DA moves to the edge and dips his hand in the water.

SON: What are you at, da? Come away from there – you'll fall. Finish the story, da.

DA: I won't fall, son… I won't do that… Can you smell it…?

SON: I can. Come away from the edge, da.

DA: The original chowder… Your mother really loved you – do you know that? She was so proud of you. And I loved you. And I will, always… And when she fell sick – and you only after leavin'… She was happy beyond everythin' you came back… And these things aren't easy to say… And you knew it…deep down you knew it…but maybe I didn't tell you it…but I felt it. I felt it every day of my life… And I hope you felt

77

something for us… I think you did – did you…? Was
I an embarrassment to you…? I'm sure I was some of
the time… But not always, I hope… And your mother,
Lord have mercy on her soul, she loved you more
than anything, and forgave you everything…that most
beautiful woman… And my God she was so proud. We
were…and are…and ever will be… So that's it! The line
goes on! Me work is done…

SON: What do you mean?

DA: She spoke to me last night.

SON: Who did…? Ah da!

DA: Told me she was lonely. She misses me, and I miss
her… As an English might say – I've had a good
innings…! And you have all my stories. I'm going to
where I belong, Thomas…

Music begins – melancholy ballad resumes.

What use is an Irishman who can't make himself a cup
of tea?

SON: I'll make you tea, da…! Will you not meet your
grandson…?

DA: I've drunk me fill.

He tests the water again.

I don't need to meet him, Thomas… It's warm too…

SON: Da…? Would you not leave that to rest?

DA: What?

SON: All that… The English, and all…

DA: You want me to forget who I am?

SON: No da.

DA: And my experience?

SON: No!

DA: Good... That's your job... Hah...? Did you fight a man last night? In the bar...?

SON doesn't respond.

I knew you didn't...but that's alright. Give us a hug!

They embrace.

Enjoy the remainder!

SON: Ahhhhhh...! Da...!

DA carefully slips into the water and out of the light.

DA: It's beautiful...! What's wrong with you?

SON: Me head's in a muddle.

DA: And who is it you're thinking of?

SON: I don't know... I don't know...! Da...? Will you tell her I was askin' for her?

DA: Askin' what?

SON: Askin' after her?

DA: Will she know what you mean?

SON: She will.

DA: I suppose she will...

SON: And I'll see her soon.

DA: I will of course... Good luck... Remember me to him!

SON: I sure will... Good luck, da... Slán...!

DA: Good man...!

Pause.

SON: How's the leg, da...?

Light begins to fade slowly. Music fades also.

Da...? How's the leg...? Da...? 'Which one,' says you...
Hah...? Da...? Da...? Da...? Da...? Da...? Da...?

THOMAS remains in the boat, with one arm, and one oar.

Music out.

The end.

WWW.OBERONBOOKS.COM

Follow us on www.twitter.com/@oberonbooks
& www.facebook.com/OberonBooksLondon

Printed in the USA
CPSIA information can be obtained
at www.ICGtesting.com
LVHW020959171024
794056LV00004B/1230